INSTRUCTION ON CERTAIN QUESTIONS REGARDING THE COLLABORATION OF THE NON-ORDAINED FAITHFUL IN THE SACRED MINISTRY OF PRIESTS

Ecclesiae de Mysterio

BOOKS & MEDIA

BOSTON

The English translation of some Latin excerpts from the Code of Canon Law is taken from the *Code of Canon Law,* © 1983, Canon Law Society of America, Washington, D.C.

Vatican Translation

ISBN 0-8198-3677-X

Printed and published in the U.S.A. by Pauline Books & Media, 50 St. Paul's Avenue, Boston, MA 02130.

http://www.pauline.org

Pauline Books & Media is the publishing house of the Daughters of St. Paul, an international congregation of women religious serving the Church with the communications media.

2 3 4 5 6 7 03 02 01 00 99 98

CONTENTS

FOREWORD

The source of the call addressed to all members of the Mystical Body to participate actively in the mission and edification of the People of God is to be found in the mystery of the Church. The People of God participate in this call through the dynamic of an organic communion in accord with their diverse ministries and charisms. The call has been forcefully repeated in the documents of the Magisterium, particularly since the Second Vatican Ecumenical Council[1] and thereafter. This is especially true of the last three General Ordinary Assemblies of the Synod of Bishops which reaffirmed the particular identities of the lay faithful and of sacred ministers and religious, in their proper dignity and diversity of functions. These assemblies encouraged all the faithful to build up the Church by collaborating, in communion, for the salvation of the world.

The necessity and importance of apostolic action on the part of the lay faithful in present and future evangelization must be borne in mind. The Church cannot put aside this task because it is part of her very nature, as the "People of God," and

1. Cf. Second Vatican Ecumenical Council, Dogmatic Constitution on the Church *Lumen Gentium,* 33; Decree *Apostolicam Actuositatem,* 24.

also because she has need of it in order to realize her own mission of evangelization.

This call for the active participation of all the faithful in the mission of the Church has not been unheard. The 1987 Synod of Bishops observed:

> The Holy Spirit continues to renew the youthfulness of the Church and has inspired new aspirations toward holiness and the participation of so many lay faithful. This is witnessed, among other ways, in the new manner of active collaboration among priests, religious and the lay faithful; by active participation in the liturgy; in the proclamation of the Word of God and catechesis; in the multiplicity of services and tasks entrusted to the lay faithful and fulfilled by them; by the flourishing of groups, associations and spiritual movements as well as by lay commitment to the life of the Church and in the fuller and meaningful participation of women in the development of society.[2]

This was likewise verified in the preparation for the 1994 Synod of Bishops on religious life where it is stated: "Through all, there should be a sincere desire to instill an authentic rapport of communion and of collaboration between the bishops, institutes of consecrated life, the secular clergy and the laity."[3] In the subsequent Post-Synodal Exhortation, the Supreme Pontiff confirmed the specific contribution of religious life in the mission and the building up of the Church.[4]

---

2. John Paul II, Post-Synodal Apostolic Exhortation *Christifideles Laici* (Dec. 30, 1988), 2: *AAS* 81 (1989), p. 396.

3. Synod of Bishops, IX General Ordinary Assembly, *Instrumentum Laboris,* 73.

4. Cf. John Paul II, Post-Synodal Apostolic Exhortation *Vita Consecrata* (Mar. 25, 1996), 47: *AAS* 88 (1996), p. 420.

In effect, a collaboration of all the faithful exists in both orders of the Church's mission; whether it is in the spiritual order, bringing the message of Christ and his grace to men, or in the temporal one, permeating and perfecting secular reality with the evangelical spirit.[5] This is especially true in the primary areas of evangelization and sanctification: "It is in this sphere most of all that the lay apostolate and the pastoral ministry complete each other."[6] In these areas, the lay faithful of both sexes have innumerable opportunities to be actively involved. This is possible through bearing consistent witness in their personal, family and social lives by proclaiming and sharing the Gospel of Christ in every situation in which they find themselves, and by their involvement with the task of explaining, defending and correctly applying Christian principles to the problems of today's world.[7] In particular, pastors are exhorted to "...acknowledge and foster the ministries, the offices and roles of the lay faithful that find their foundation in the sacraments of Baptism and Confirmation, indeed for a good many of them, in the sacrament of Matrimony."[8]

The present reality is that there has been an astonishing growth of pastoral initiatives in this area. This is especially true after the notable impetus given by the Second Vatican Council and the pontifical Magisterium in this regard.

The priority of the task of the new evangelization, which

---

5. Cf. Second Vatican Ecumenical Council, Decree *Apostolicam Actuositatem,* 5.

6. *Ibid.,* 6.

7. Cf. *ibid.*

8. John Paul II, Post-Synodal Apostolic Exhortation *Christifideles Laici* (Dec. 30, 1988), 23: *AAS* 81 (1989), p. 429.

involves all the People of God, requires that, today in particular, in addition to a "special activism" on the part of priests, there be also a full recovery of the awareness of the secular nature of the mission of the laity.[9]

This enterprise opens vast horizons, some of which have yet to be explored, for the lay faithful. The faithful can be active in this particular moment of history in areas of culture, in the arts and theater, scientific research, labor, means of communication, politics, the economy, etc. They are also called to a greater creativity in seeking out ever more effective means whereby these environments can find the fullness of their meaning in Christ.[10]

In this great field of complementary activity, whether considering the specifically spiritual and religious, or the *consecratio mundi,* there exists a more restricted area, namely, the sacred ministry of the clergy. In this ministry the lay faithful, men or women and non-ordained members of institutes of consecrated life and societies of apostolic life, are called to assist. The Second Vatican Ecumenical Council refers particularly to this when it teaches: "The hierarchy entrusts the laity with certain charges more closely connected with the duties of pastors: in the teaching of Christian doctrine, for example, in certain liturgical actions in the care of souls."[11]

---

9. Cf. Second Vatican Ecumenical Council, Dogmatic Constitution *Lumen Gentium,* 31; John Paul II, Post-Synodal Apostolic Exhortation *Christifideles Laici,* 15, *loc. cit.*, pp. 413-416.

10. Cf. Second Vatican Ecumenical Council, Pastoral Constitution *Gaudium et Spes,* 43.

11. Second Vatican Ecumenical Council, Decree *Apostolicam Actuositatem,* 24.

Since these tasks are most closely linked to the duties of pastors (which office requires reception of the sacrament of Orders), it is necessary that all who are in any way involved in this collaboration exercise particular care to safeguard the nature and mission of sacred ministry and the vocation and secular character of the lay faithful. It must be remembered that "collaboration with" does not, in fact, mean "substitution for."

It must be noted with great satisfaction that in many particular Churches the collaboration of the non-ordained faithful in the pastoral ministry of the clergy has developed in a very positive fashion. It has borne an abundance of good fruits, while at the same time being mindful of the boundaries established by the nature of the sacraments and of the diversity of charisms and ecclesiastical functions. It has also brought about bounteous and tangible results in situations of a shortage or scarcity of sacred ministers.[12] In situations of emergency and chronic necessity in certain communities, some of the faithful, despite lacking the character of the sacrament of Orders, have acted appropriately and within their proper limits in dealing with these realities. The necessary aspect of hierarchical relationship has been maintained while constantly seeking to remedy the situation of emergency.[13] Such faithful are called and deputed to assume specific duties which are as important as they are sensitive. Sustained by the grace of the Lord and by

---

12. Cf. John Paul II, Discourse at the Symposium on "The Participation of the Lay Faithful in the Priestly Ministry" (April 22, 1994), 2, *L'Osservatore Romano,* English Edition, May 11, 1994.

13. Cf. *C.I.C.,* canons 230, § 3; 517, § 2; 861, § 2; 910, § 2; 943; 1112; John Paul II, Post-Synodal Apostolic Exhortation *Christifideles Laici* (Dec. 30, 1988), 23 and note 72: *AAS* 81 (1989), p. 430.

their sacred ministers journeying alongside them, they are well received by the communities which they serve. Sacred pastors are extremely grateful for the generosity with which numerous religious and lay faithful present themselves for this specific service, carried out with a loyal *"sensus Ecclesiae"* and an edifying dedication. Particular thanks and encouragement should be extended to those who carry out these tasks in situations of persecution of the Christian community. This is also true for mission territories, whether these be geographical or cultural, and for places where the Church is newly planted or where the presence of the priest is only sporadic.[14]

This is not the place to develop the theological and pastoral richness of the role of the lay faithful in the Church, which has already been amply treated in the Apostolic Exhortation *Christifideles Laici.*

The scope of this present document is simply to provide a clear, authoritative response to the many pressing requests which have come to our dicasteries from bishops, priests and laity seeking clarification in the light of specific cases of new forms of "pastoral activity" of the non-ordained on both parochial and diocesan levels.

Though being born in very difficult and emergency situations and even initiated by those who sought to be genuinely helpful in the pastoral moment, certain practices have often been developed which have had very serious negative consequences and have caused the correct understanding of true ecclesial communion to be damaged. These practices tend to

14. Cf. John Paul II, Encyclical Letter *Redemptoris Missio* (Dec. 7, 1990), 37: *AAS* 83 (1991), pp. 282-286.

predominate in certain areas of the world and even within these, a great deal of variation can be found.

These matters cause the grave pastoral responsibility of many to be recalled. This is especially true of bishops,[15] whose task it is to promote and ensure observance of the universal discipline of the Church, founded on certain doctrinal principles already clearly enunciated by the Second Vatican Ecumenical Council[16] and by the pontifical Magisterium[17] thereafter.

This document came into being as a result of deliberations within our dicasteries as well as from a symposium attended by representatives of the episcopates most affected by the problem. Finally, there was an extensive consultation of many presidents of conferences of bishops, of individual prelates, as well as with experts from the various ecclesiastical disciplines and from different parts of the world. From all of the foregoing, a clear convergence emerged which is faithfully presented in this instruction. However, the document does not claim to be exhaustive nor can it address every possible variation which might present itself. It is limited to consideration of the best known of these, as there is a great variety of particular circumstances possible which can give rise to these situations.

This text was drawn up based on the solid foundation of the ordinary and extraordinary Magisterium of the Church, and is entrusted for its faithful application first of all to the bishops

---

15. Cf. *C.I.C.,* canon 392.

16. Cf. especially Second Vatican Ecumenical Council, Dogmatic Constitution *Lumen Gentium,* Constitution *Sacrosanctum Concilium,* Decree *Presbyterorum Ordinis* and Decree *Apostolicam Actuositatem.*

17. Cf. especially Apostolic Exhortations *Christifideles Laici* and *Pastores Dabo Vobis.*

most affected by the issues raised. It is also brought to the attention of the prelates of those ecclesiastical jurisdictions where, even though the practices described are not found in those territories at this time, given their rapid diffusion, such situations could change quickly.

Before addressing the concrete situations which were presented to us, it is necessary to look briefly at the essential theological elements underlying the significance of Holy Orders in the organic makeup of the Church. This is so that the ecclesiastical discipline will be understood better in light of the truth and of ecclesial communion, which are concerned with promoting the rights and obligations of all, and for which in the Church "the salvation of souls must always be the supreme law."[18]

18. Cf. canon 1752.

THEOLOGICAL PRINCIPLES

1. The Common Priesthood of the Faithful and the Ministerial Priesthood

Jesus Christ, the Eternal High Priest, wished that his one and indivisible priesthood be transmitted to his Church. This Church is the people of the New Covenant who, "through Baptism and the anointing of the Holy Spirit are reborn and consecrated as a spiritual temple and a holy priesthood. By living the Christian life, they offer up spiritual sacrifices and proclaim the prodigious deeds of him who called them from darkness into his own wonderful light (cf. 1 Pt 2:4-10)."[19] "There is but one chosen People of God: 'one Lord, one faith, one Baptism' (Eph 4:5): there is a common dignity of members deriving from their rebirth in Christ, a common grace of filial adoption, a common vocation to perfection."[20] There exists "a true equality between all with regard to the dignity and to the activity which is common to all the faithful in building up the

19. Cf. Second Vatican Ecumenical Council, Dogmatic Constitution *Lumen Gentium,* 10.

20. *Ibid.*, 32.

body of Christ." By the will of Christ some are constituted "teachers, dispensers of the mysteries, and pastors."[21] The common priesthood of the faithful and the ministerial or hierarchical priesthood "though they differ essentially and not only in degree...are nonetheless ordered one to another; [since] each in its own proper way shares in the one priesthood of Christ."[22] Between both there is an effective unity since the Holy Spirit makes the Church one in communion, in service and in the outpouring of the diverse hierarchical and charismatic gifts.[23]

Thus the essential difference between the common priesthood of the faithful and the ministerial priesthood is not found in the priesthood of Christ, which remains forever one and indivisible, nor in the sanctity to which all of the faithful are called: "Indeed the ministerial priesthood does not of itself signify a greater degree of holiness with regard to the common priesthood of the faithful; through it, Christ gives to priests, in the Spirit, a particular gift so that they can help the People of God to exercise faithfully and fully the common priesthood which it has received."[24] "For the building up of the Church, the Body of Christ, there is a diversity of members and functions but only one Spirit who, for the good of the Church, distributes his various gifts with munificence proportionate to his riches and the needs of service (cf. 1 Cor 12:1-11)."[25]

---

21. *Ibid.*

22. *Ibid.,* 10.

23. Cf. *ibid.,* 4.

24. John Paul II, Post-Synodal Apostolic Exhortation *Pastores Dabo Vobis* (Mar. 25, 1992), 17: *AAS* 84 (1992), p. 684.

25. Cf. Second Vatican Ecumenical Council, Dogmatic Constitution *Lumen Gentium,* 7.

This diversity exists at the *mode* of participation in the priesthood of Christ and is essential in the sense that "while the common priesthood of the faithful is exercised by the unfolding of baptismal grace—a life of faith, hope and charity, a life according to the Spirit—the ministerial priesthood is at the service of the common priesthood. It is directed at the unfolding of the baptismal grace of all Christians."[26] Consequently, the ministerial priesthood "differs in essence from the common priesthood of the faithful because it confers a sacred power for the service of the faithful."[27] For this reason the priest is exhorted "...to grow in awareness of the deep communion uniting him to the People of God" in order to "awaken and deepen co-responsibility in the one common mission of salvation, with a prompt and heartfelt esteem for all the charisms and tasks which the Spirit gives believers for the building up of the Church."[28]

The characteristics which differentiate the ministerial priesthood of bishops and priests from the common priesthood of the faithful, and consequently delineate the extent to which other members of the faithful cooperate with this ministry, may be summarized in the following fashion:

a) the ministerial priesthood is rooted in the apostolic succession, and vested with "*potestas sacra,*"[29] consisting of the

26. *Catechism of the Catholic Church,* 1547.

27. *Ibid.,* 1592.

28. John Paul II, Post-Synodal Apostolic Exhortation *Pastores Dabo Vobis* (Mar. 25, 1992), 74: *AAS* 84 (1992), p. 788.

29. Cf. Second Vatican Ecumenical Council, Dogmatic Constitution *Lumen Gentium,* 10, 18, 27, 28; the Decree *Presbyterorum Ordinis,* 2, 6; *Catechism of the Catholic Church,* 1538, 1576.

faculty and the responsibility of acting in the person of Christ the Head and the Shepherd;[30]

b) it is a priesthood which renders its sacred ministers servants of Christ and of the Church by means of authoritative proclamation of the Word of God, the administration of the sacraments and the pastoral direction of the faithful.[31]

To base the foundations of the ordained ministry on apostolic succession, because this ministry continues the mission received by the apostles from Christ, is an essential point of Catholic ecclesiological doctrine.[32]

The ordained ministry, therefore, is established on the foundation of the apostles for the upbuilding of the Church,[33] "and is completely at the service of the Church."[34] "Intrinsically linked to the sacramental nature of ecclesial ministry is its *character as service.* Entirely dependent on Christ who gives mission and authority, ministers are truly 'servants of Christ' (Rom 1:1) in the image of him who freely took 'the form of a slave' (Phil 2:7) for us. Because the word and grace of which

---

30. Cf. John Paul II, Post-Synodal Apostolic Exhortation *Pastores Dabo Vobis* (Mar. 25, 1992), 15: *AAS* 84 (1992), p. 680; *Catechism of the Catholic Church*, 875.

31. Cf. John Paul II, Post-Synodal Apostolic Exhortation *Pastores Dabo Vobis,* 16: *loc. cit.*, pp. 681-684; *Catechism of the Catholic Church,* 1592.

32. Cf. John Paul II, Post-Synodal Apostolic Exhortation *Pastores Dabo Vobis,* 14-16: *loc. cit.*, pp. 678-684; Congregation for the Doctrine of the Faith, Letter *Sacerdotum Ministeriale* (Aug. 6, 1983), III, 2-3: *AAS* 75 (1983), pp. 1004-1005.

33. Cf. Eph 2:20; Rev 21:14.

34. John Paul II, Post-Synodal Apostolic Exhortation *Pastores Dabo Vobis* (Mar. 25, 1992), 16: *AAS* 84 (1992), p. 681.

they are ministers are not their own, but are given to them by Christ for the sake of others, they must freely become the slaves of all."[35]

2. Unity and Diversity of Ministerial Functions

The functions of the ordained minister, taken as a whole, constitute a single indivisible unity in virtue of their singular foundation in Christ.[36] As with Christ,[37] salvific activity is one and unique. It is signified and realized by the minister through the functions of teaching, sanctifying and governing the faithful. This unity essentially defines the exercise of the sacred minister's functions which are always an exercise, in different ways, of the role of Christ as Head of the Church.

Therefore, since the exercise of the *munus docendi, sanctificandi et regendi* by the sacred minister constitutes the essence of pastoral ministry, the diverse functions proper to ordained ministers form an indivisible unity and cannot be understood if separated one from the other. Rather they must be viewed in terms of mutual correspondence and complementarity. Only in some of these functions, and to a limited degree, may the non-ordained faithful cooperate with their pastors should they be called to do so by lawful authority and in accordance with the prescribed manner. "He [Jesus Christ] continually provides in his body, that is, in the Church, for gifts of ministries through

35. *Catechism of the Catholic Church*, 876.

36. Cf. *ibid.*, 1581.

37. Cf. John Paul II, Letter *Novo Incipiente* (April 8, 1979), 3: *AAS* 71 (1979), p. 397.

which, by his power, we serve each other unto salvation...."[38] "*The exercise of such tasks does not make pastors of the lay faithful,* in fact, a person is not a minister simply in performing a task, but through sacramental ordination. Only the sacrament of Orders gives the ordained minister a particular participation in the office of Christ, the Shepherd and Head in his eternal priesthood. The task exercised in virtue of supply takes its legitimacy formally and immediately from the official deputation given by pastors, as well as from its concrete exercise under the guidance of ecclesiastical authority."[39]

This doctrine needs to be reaffirmed especially in the light of certain practices which seek to compensate for numerical shortages of ordained ministers arising in some communities. In some instances, such have given rise to an idea of the common priesthood of the faithful which mistakes its nature and specific meaning. Among other things, it can encourage a reduction in vocations to the (ministerial) priesthood and obscure the specific purpose of seminaries as places of formation for the ordained ministry. These are closely related phenomena. Their interdependence calls for careful reflection so as to arrive at well considered conclusions in their regard.

3. The Indispensability of the Ordained Ministry

For a community of the faithful to be called a Church, and indeed to truly be a Church, it cannot be guided according to political criteria or those of human organizations. Every par-

---

38. Second Vatican Ecumenical Council, Dogmatic Constitution *Lumen Gentium*, 7.

39. John Paul II, Post-Synodal Apostolic Exhortation *Christifideles Laici* (Dec. 30, 1998), 23: *AAS* 81 (1989), p. 430.

ticular Church *owes* its guidance to Christ, since it was he who fundamentally linked apostolic mission to the Church, and hence no community has the power to grant that mission to itself[40] or to delegate it. In effect, a canonical or juridical determination made by hierarchical authority is necessary for the exercise of the *munus* of teaching and governing.[41]

The ministerial priesthood is therefore necessary for a community to exist as "Church": "The ordained priesthood ought not to be thought of as existing...posterior to the ecclesial community, as if the Church could be imagined as already established without this priesthood."[42] Indeed, were a community to lack a priest, it would be deprived of the exercise and sacramental action of Christ, the Head and Pastor, which are essential for the very life of every ecclesial community.

Thus the ordained priesthood is absolutely irreplaceable. As an immediate consequence of this there is the necessity for a continuing, zealous and well-organized pastoral promotion of vocations so as to provide the Church with those ministers which she needs and to ensure a proper seminary training for those preparing for the sacrament of Holy Orders. Any other solution to problems deriving from a shortage of sacred ministers can only lead to precarious consequences.

"The duty of fostering vocations falls on the whole Christian community, and they should discharge it principally by

---

40. Cf. Congregation for the Doctrine of the Faith, Letter *Sacerdotium Ministeriale,* III, 2: *loc. cit.*, p. 1004.

41. Cf. Second Vatican Ecumenical Council, Dogmatic Constitution *Lumen Gentium, Nota explicativa praevia,* 2.

42. John Paul II, Post-Synodal Apostolic Exhortation *Pastores Dabo Vobis,* 16: *loc. cit.*, p. 682.

living full Christian lives."[43] By following Christ more closely and in overcoming indifference, all the faithful have a responsibility to foster a positive response to priestly vocation. This is especially true for those nations where a strong sense of materialism is evident.

4. The Collaboration of the Non-Ordained Faithful in Pastoral Ministry

Among the various aspects of the participation of the non-ordained faithful in the Church's mission considered by the conciliar documents, that of their direct collaboration with the ministry of the Church's pastors is considered.[44] Indeed, "when necessity and expediency in the Church require it, the pastors, according to established norms from universal law, can entrust to the lay faithful certain offices and roles that are connected to their pastoral ministry but do not require the character of Orders."[45] In this way, it is not one merely of assistance but of mutual enrichment of the common Christian vocation. This collaboration was regulated by successive post-conciliar legislation and particularly by the *Codex Iuris Canonici*.

The Code, having referred to the rights and duties of all the faithful,[46] in the subsequent title devoted to the rights and duties of the lay faithful, treats not only of those which are

43. Second Vatican Ecumenical Council, Decree *Optatam Totius,* 2.

44. Cf. Second Vatican Ecumenical Council, Decree *Apostolicam Actuositatem,* 24.

45. John Paul II, Post-Synodal Apostolic Exhortation *Christifideles Laici* (Dec. 30, 1988), 23: *AAS* 81 (1989), p. 429.

46. Cf. *C.I.C.*, canons 208-223.

theirs in virtue of their secular condition,[47] but also of those tasks and functions which are not exclusively theirs. Some of these latter refer to any member of the faithful, whether ordained or not,[48] while others are considered along the lines of collaboration with the sacred ministry of cleric.[49] With regard to these last mentioned areas or functions, the non-ordained faithful do not enjoy a right to such tasks and functions. Rather, they are "capable of being admitted by the sacred pastors...to those functions which, in accordance with the provisions of law, they can discharge"[50] or where "ministers are not available...they can supply certain of their functions...in accordance with the provisions of law."[51]

To ensure that such collaboration is harmoniously incorporated into pastoral ministry, and to avoid situations of abuse and disciplinary irregularity in pastoral practice, it is always necessary to have clarity in doctrinal principles. Therefore a consistent, faithful and serious application of the current canonical dispositions throughout the entire Church, while avoiding the abuse of multiplying "exceptional" cases over and above those so designated and regulated by normative discipline, is extremely necessary.

Where the existence of abuses or improper practices has been proved, pastors will promptly employ those means judged

---

47. Cf. *ibid.*, canons 225, § 2; 226; 227; 231, § 2.

48. Cf. *ibid.*, canons 225, § 1; 228, § 2; 229; 231, § 1.

49. Cf. *ibid.*, canons 230, §§ 2-3, for that which pertains to the liturgy; canon 228, § 1 in relation to other areas of sacred ministry; the last paragraph applies to other areas outside the ministry of clerics.

50. *Ibid.*, canon 228, § 1.

51. *Ibid.*, canons 230, § 3; cf. 517, § 2; 776; 861, § 2; 910, § 2; 943; 1112.

necessary to prevent their dissemination and to ensure that the correct understanding of the Church's nature is not impaired. In particular, they will apply the established disciplinary norms to promote knowledge of and assiduous respect for that distinction and complementarity of functions which are vital for ecclesial communion. Where abusive practices have become widespread, it is absolutely necessary for those who exercise authority to intervene responsibly so as to promote communion, which can only be done by adherence to the truth. Communion, truth, justice, peace and charity are all interdependent terms.[52]

In the light of the aforementioned principles, remedies based on the normative discipline of the Church and deemed opportune to correct abuses which have been brought to the attention of our dicasteries, are hereby set forth.

---

52. Cf. Sacred Congregation for Divine Worship and the Discipline of the Sacraments, foreword of the Instruction *Inaestimabile Donum* (April 3, 1980), *AAS* 72 (1980), pp. 331-333.

PRACTICAL PROVISIONS

ARTICLE 1

Need for an Appropriate Terminology

In his address to participants at the Symposium on "Collaboration of the Lay Faithful with the Priestly Ministry," the Holy Father emphasized the need to clarify and distinguish the various meanings which have accrued to the term "ministry" in theological and canonical language.[53]

§ 1. "For some time now, it has been customary to use the word *ministries* not only for the *officia (offices)* and non-ordained *munera (functions)* exercised by pastors in virtue of the sacrament of Orders, but also for those exercised by the lay faithful in virtue of their baptismal priesthood. The terminological question becomes even more complex and delicate when all the faithful are recognized as having the possibility of supplying—by official deputation given by the pastors—certain

53. Cf. John Paul II, Discourse at the Symposium on "The Participation of the Lay Faithful in the Priestly Ministry" (April 22, 1994), 3, *L'Osservatore Romano*, English Edition, May 11, 1994.

functions more proper to clerics, which, nevertheless, do not require the character of Orders. It must be admitted that the language becomes doubtful, confused, and hence not helpful for expressing the doctrine of the faith whenever the difference 'of essence and not merely of degree' between the baptismal priesthood and the ordained priesthood is in any way obscured."[54]

§ 2. "In some cases, the extension of the term 'ministry' to the *munera* belonging to the lay faithful has been permitted by the fact that the latter, to their own degree, are a participation in the one priesthood of Christ. The *officia* temporarily entrusted to them, however, are exclusively the result of a deputation by the Church. Only with constant reference to the one source, the 'ministry of Christ'...may the term *ministry* be applied to a certain extent and without ambiguity to the lay faithful: that is, without it being perceived and lived as an undue aspiration to the *ordained ministry* or as a progressive erosion of its specific nature.

"In this original sense the term *ministry (servitium)* expresses only the work by which the Church's members continue the mission and ministry of Christ within her and the whole world. However, when the term is distinguished from and compared with the various *munera* and *officia,* then it should be clearly noted that *only* in virtue of sacred ordination does the work obtain that full, univocal meaning that tradition has attributed to it."[55]

---

54. *Ibid.*

55. Cf. John Paul II, Discourse at the Symposium on "The Participation of the Lay Faithful in the Priestly Ministry" (April 22, 1994), 3, *L'Osservatore Romano,* English Edition, May 11, 1994.

§ 3. The non-ordained faithful may be generically designated "extraordinary ministers" when deputed by competent authority to discharge, solely by way of supply, those offices mentioned in canon 230, § 3[56] and in canons 943 and 1112. Naturally, the concrete term may be applied to those to whom functions are canonically entrusted, e.g., catechists, acolytes, lectors, etc.

Temporary deputation for liturgical purposes—mentioned in canon 230, § 2—does not confer any special or permanent title on the non-ordained faithful.[57]

It is unlawful for the non-ordained faithful to assume titles such as "pastor," "chaplain," "coordinator," "moderator" or other such similar titles which can confuse their role and that of the pastor, who is always a bishop or priest.[58]

---

56. Cf. Pontifical Commission for the Authentic Interpretation of the Code of Canon Law, *Response* (June 1, 1988): *AAS* 80 (1988), p. 1373.

57. Cf. Pontifical Council for the Interpretation of Legislative Texts, *Response* (July 11, 1992): *AAS* 86 (1994), pp. 541-542. Any ceremony associated with the deputation of the non-ordained as collaborators in the ministry of clerics must not have any semblance to the ceremony of sacred ordination, nor may such a ceremony have a form analogous to that of the conferral of lector or acolyte.

58. Such examples should include all those linguistic expressions which in languages of the various countries are similar or equal, and indicate a directive role of leadership or such vicarious activity.

Article 2

The Ministry of the Word[59]

§ 1. The content of that ministry consists in "the pastoral preaching, catechetics and all forms of Christian instruction, among which the liturgical homily should hold pride of place."[60]

The exercise of its respective functions is properly that of the bishop of each particular Church since he is the moderator of the entire ministry of the Word in his diocese,[61] and it is also properly that of his priests who are his collaborators.[62] In communion with the bishop and his priests, this ministry also belongs to deacons.[63]

§ 2. The non-ordained faithful, according to their proper character, participate in the prophetic function of Christ, are constituted as his witnesses and afforded the *"sensus fidei"* and the grace of the Word. All are called to grow even more as "heralds of faith in things to be hoped for" (cf. Heb 11:1).[64] Today, much depends on their commitment and generous service to the Church, especially in the work of catechesis.

---

59. For the different forms of preaching, cf. *C.I.C.*, canon 761; *Missale Romanum, Ordo Lectionum Missae,* Praenotanda: ed. Typica Altera, 1981.

60. Second Vatican Ecumenical Council, Dogmatic Constitution *Dei Verbum,* 24.

61. Cf. *C.I.C.,* canon 756, § 2.

62. Cf. *ibid.,* canon 757.

63. Cf. *ibid.*

64. Second Vatican Ecumenical Council, Dogmatic Constitution *Lumen Gentium,* 35.

Therefore, the faithful, especially members of institutes of consecrated life and societies of apostolic life, can be invited to collaborate, in lawful ways, in the exercise of the ministry of the Word.[65]

§ 3. To ensure the effectiveness of the collaboration mentioned in § 2 above, it is necessary to note some conditions relating to the operation of this same collaboration.

Canon 766 of the *Codex Iuris Canonici* establishes the conditions under which competent authority may admit the non-ordained faithful to preach *in ecclesia vel oratorio* [in a church or oratory]. The use of the expression *admitti possunt* [can be admitted] makes clear that in no instance is this a right such as that which is specific and proper to the bishop[66] or a faculty such as enjoyed by priests and deacons.[67]

The terms in which these conditions are expressed—"If in certain circumstances it is *necessary*...; ...if in particular cases it would be *useful*..."—in canon 766, make clear the exceptional nature of such cases as well as the fact that such must always be done *iuxta episcoporum conferentiae praescripta* [according to the prescriptions of the conference of bishops]. In this final clause, this canon establishes the primary source for correct discernment with regard to *necessity* or *useful* in specific cases. The prescriptions of the conference of bishops in this matter, which must receive the *"recognitio"* of the Apostolic See, are

65. Cf. *C.I.C.*, canons 758-759; 785, § 1.

66. Cf. Second Vatican Ecumenical Council, Dogmatic Constitution *Lumen Gentium*, 25; *C.I.C.*, canon 763.

67. Cf. *C.I.C.*, canon 764.

obliged to lay down those opportune criteria which may assist the diocesan bishop in making appropriate pastoral decisions, proper to the nature of the same episcopal office.

§ 4. In some areas, circumstances can arise in which a shortage of sacred ministers and permanent, objectively verifiable, situations of need or advantage exist that would recommend the admission of the non-ordained faithful to preaching.

Preaching in churches or oratories by the non-ordained faithful can be permitted only as a *supply* for sacred ministers or for those particular reasons foreseen by the universal law of the Church or by conferences of bishops. It cannot, however, be regarded as an ordinary occurrence nor as an authentic promotion of the laity.

§ 5. Above all in the preparation for the sacraments, catechists take care to instruct those being catechized on the role and figure of the priest as the sole dispenser of the mysteries for which they are preparing.

ARTICLE 3

The Homily

§ 1. The homily, being an eminent form of preaching—*qua per anni liturgici cursum ex textu sacro fidei mysteria et normae vitae christianae exponuntia*[68] [the mysteries of faith and the norms of Christian living are to be expounded from the sacred text throughout the course of the liturgical year]—also forms part of the liturgy.

---

68. *C.I.C.,* canon 767, § 1; cf. Second Vatican Ecumenical Council, Constitution *Sacrosanctum Concilium,* 53-55.

The homily, therefore, during the celebration of the Holy Eucharist, must be reserved to the sacred minister, priest or deacon[69] to the exclusion of the non-ordained faithful, even if these should have responsibilities as "pastoral assistants" or catechists in whatever type of community or group. This exclusion is not based on the preaching ability of sacred ministers nor their theological preparation, but on that function which is reserved to them in virtue of having received the sacrament of Holy Orders. For the same reason the diocesan bishop cannot validly dispense from the canonical norm[70] since this is not merely a disciplinary law but one which touches upon the closely connected functions of teaching and sanctifying.

For the same reason, the practice, on some occasions, of entrusting the preaching of the homily to seminarians or theology students who are not clerics[71] is not permitted. Indeed, the homily should not be regarded as a training for some future ministry.

---

69. Cf. John Paul II, Apostolic Exhortation *Catechesi Tradendae* (Oct. 16, 1979), 48: *AAS* 71 (1979), pp. 1277-1340; Pontifical Commission for Interpreting the Decrees of the Second Vatican Ecumenical Council, *Response* (Jan. 11, 1971): *AAS* 63 (1971), p. 329; Sacred Congregation for Divine Worship, Instruction *Actio Pastoralis* (May 15, 1969) 6d: *AAS* 61 (1969), p. 809; *Institutio Generalis Missalis Romani* (Mar. 26, 1970), nn. 41, 42, 165; the Instruction *Liturgicae Instaurationes* (Sept. 15, 1970), 2a: *AAS* 62 (1970), p. 696; Sacred Congregation for the Sacraments and Divine Worship, Instruction *Inaestimabile Donum* (April 3, 1980), 3: *AAS* 72 (1980), p. 331.

70. Pontifical Council for the Authentic Interpretation of the Code of Canon Law, *Response* (June 20, 1987): *AAS* 79 (1987), p. 1249.

71. Cf. *C.I.C.*, canon 266, § 1.

All previous norms which may have admitted the non-ordained faithful to preaching the homily during the Holy Eucharist are to be considered abrogated by canon 767, § 1.[72]

§ 2. A form of instruction designed to promote a greater understanding of the liturgy, including personal testimonies, or the celebration of Eucharistic liturgies on special occasions (e.g. day of the seminary, day of the sick, etc.) is lawful, if in harmony with liturgical norms, should such be considered objectively opportune as a means of explicating the regular homily preached by the celebrant priest. Nonetheless, these testimonies or explanations may not be such so as to assume a character which could be confused with the homily.

§ 3. As an expositional aide and providing it does not delegate the duty of preaching to others, the celebrant minister may make prudent use of "dialogue" in the homily, in accord with the liturgical norms.[73]

§ 4. Homilies in non-Eucharistic liturgies may be preached by the non-ordained faithful only when expressly permitted by law and when its prescriptions for doing so are observed.

§ 5. In no instance may the homily be entrusted to priests or deacons who have lost the clerical state or who have abandoned the sacred ministry.[74]

---

72. Cf. *ibid.*, canon 6, § 1, 2°.

73. Cf. Sacred Congregation for Divine Worship, Directory for Masses with Children *Pueros Baptizatos* (Nov. 1, 1973), 48: *AAS* 66 (1974), p. 44.

74. For information on priests who have obtained a dispensation from celibacy, cf. the Sacred Congregation for the Doctrine of the Faith, *Normae de Dispensatione a Sacerdotali Coelibatu ad Instantiam Partis* (Oct. 14, 1980), "Normae substantialis," art. 5.

Article 4

The Parish Priest and the Parish

The non-ordained faithful, as happens in many worthy cases, may collaborate effectively in the pastoral ministry of clerics in parishes, health care centers, charitable and educational institutions, prisons, military ordinariates, etc. Provisions regulating such extraordinary form of collaboration are provided by canon 517, § 2.

§ 1. The right understanding and application of this canon, according to which *"si ob sacerdotum penuriam episcopus dioecesanus aestimaverit participationem in exercitio curae pastoralis paroeciae concredendam esse diacono aliive personae sacerdotali charactere non insignite aut personarum communitati, sacerdotem constitat aliquem qui, potestatibus et facultatibus parochi instructus, curam pastoralem moderetur"* [if the diocesan bishop should decide that due to a dearth of priests a participation in the exercise of the pastoral care of a parish is to be entrusted to a deacon or to some other person who is not a priest or to a community of persons, he is to appoint some priest endowed with the powers and faculties of a pastor to supervise the pastoral care], requires that this exceptional provision be used only with strict adherence to conditions contained in it. These are:

a) ob sacerdotum penuriam [due to a dearth of priests] and not for reasons of convenience or ambiguous "advancement of the laity," etc.;

b) this is *participatio in exercitio curae pastoralis* [participation in the exercise of the pastoral care] and not directing, coordinating, moderating or governing the parish; these competencies, according to the canon, are the competencies of a priest alone.

Because these are exceptional cases, before employing them, other possibilities should be availed of, such as using the services of retired priests still capable of such service, or entrusting several parishes to one priest or to a *coetus sacerdotum*[75] [a team of several priests].

In any event, the preference which this canon gives to deacons cannot be overlooked.

The same canon, however, reaffirms that these forms of participation in the pastoral care of parishes cannot, in any way, replace the office of parish priest. The same canon decrees that *"episcopus dioecesanus...sacerdotem constituat aliquem qui potestatibus et facultatibus parochi instructus, curam pastoralem moderetur"* [the diocesan bishop...is to appoint some priest endowed with the powers and faculties of a pastor to supervise the pastoral care]. Indeed, the office of parish priest can be assigned validly only to a priest (cf. canon 521, § 1) even in cases where there is a shortage of clergy.[76]

§ 2. In the same regard, it must be noted that the parish priest is the pastor proper to the parish entrusted to him[77] and remains such until his pastoral office shall have ceased.[78]

The presentation of resignation at the age of seventy-five by a parish priest does not of itself *(ipso iure)* terminate his

75. Cf. *C.I.C.,* canon 517, § 1.

76. The non-ordained faithful or a group of them entrusted with a collaboration in the exercise of pastoral care cannot be given the title of "community leader" or any other expression indicating the same idea.

77. Cf. *C.I.C.,* canon 519.

78. Cf. *ibid.,* canon 538, §§ 1-2.

pastoral office. Such takes effect only when the diocesan bishop, following prudent consideration of all the circumstances, shall have definitively accepted his resignation in accordance with canon 538, § 3 and communicated such to him in writing.[79] In the light of those situations where scarcity of priests exists, the use of special prudence in this matter would be judicious.

In view of the right of every cleric to exercise the ministry proper to him, and in the absence of any grave health or disciplinary reasons, it should be noted that having reached the age of seventy-five does not constitute a binding reason for the diocesan bishop to accept a parish priest's resignation. This also serves to avoid a functional concept of the sacred ministry.[80]

Article 5

The Structures of Collaboration in the Particular Church

These structures, so necessary to that ecclesial renewal called for by the Second Vatican Council, have produced many positive results and have been codified in canonical legislation. They represent a form of active participation in the life and mission of the Church as communion.

§ 1. The norms of the Code with regard to the *council of priests (presbyteral council)* specifies those priests who can be its members.[81] Because the council of priests is founded on the

---

79. Cf. *ibid.,* canon 186.

80. Cf. Congregation for the Clergy, Directory for the Life and Ministry of Priests, *Tota Ecclesia* (Jan. 31, 1994), 44.

81. Cf. *C.I.C.,* canons 497-498.

common participation of the bishop and his priests in the same priesthood and ministry, membership in it is reserved to priests alone.[82]

Deacons, non-ordained members of the faithful, even if collaborators with the sacred ministers, and those priests who have lost the clerical state or who have abandoned the sacred ministry do not have either an active or a passive voice in the council of priests.

§ 2. Diocesan and parochial *pastoral councils*[83] and *parochial finance councils,*[84] of which non-ordained faithful are members, enjoy a consultative vote only and cannot in any way become deliberative structures. Only those faithful who possess the qualities prescribed by the canonical norms[85] may be elected to such responsibilities.

§ 3. It is for the parish priest to preside at parochial councils. They are to be considered invalid, and hence null and void, any deliberations entered into (or decisions taken), by a parochial council which has not been presided over by the parish priest or which has assembled contrary to his wishes.[86]

§ 4. Diocesan councils may properly and validly express their consent to an act of the bishop only in those cases in which the law expressly requires such consent.

---

82. Cf. Second Vatican Ecumenical Council, Decree *Presbyterorum Ordinis*, 7.

83. Cf. *C.I.C.*, canons 514, 536.

84. Cf. *ibid.*, canon 537.

85. Cf. *ibid.*, canon 512, §§ 1 and 3; *Catechism of the Catholic Church*, 1650.

86. Cf. *C.I.C.*, canon 536.

§ 5. Given the local situation, ordinaries may avail themselves of special study groups or of groups of experts to examine particular questions. Such groups, however, cannot be constituted as structures parallel to diocesan presbyteral or pastoral councils, nor indeed to those diocesan structures regulated by the universal law of the Church in canons 536, § 1 and 537.[87] Neither may such a group deprive these structures of their lawful authority. Where structures of this kind have arisen in the past because of local custom or through special circumstances, those measures deemed necessary to conform such structures to the current universal law of the Church must be taken.

§ 6. The *vicars forane,* sometimes called deans, archpriests, or by suchlike titles, and those called "assistant vicars," "assistant dean," etc., must always be priests.[88] The non-ordained faithful cannot be validly appointed to these offices.

ARTICLE 6

Liturgical Celebrations

§ 1. Liturgical actions must always clearly manifest the unity of the People of God as a structured communion.[89] Thus there exists a close link between the ordered exercise of liturgical action and the reflection in the liturgy of the Church's structured nature.

87. Cf. *ibid.*, canon 135, § 2.

88. Cf. *ibid.*, canon 553, § 1.

89. Cf. Second Vatican Ecumenical Council, Constitution *Sacrosanctum Concilium*, 26-28; *C.I.C.*, canon 837.

This happens when all participants, with faith and devotion, discharge those roles proper to them.

§ 2. To promote the proper identity (of various roles) in this area, those abuses which are contrary to the provisions of canon 907 are to be eradicated. In Eucharistic celebrations, deacons and non-ordained members of the faithful may not pronounce prayers—e.g., especially the Eucharistic prayer, with its concluding doxology—or any other parts of the liturgy reserved to the celebrant priest. Neither may deacons or non-ordained members of the faithful use gestures or actions which are proper to the same priest celebrant. It is a grave abuse for any member of the non-ordained faithful to "quasi preside" at the Mass while leaving only that minimal participation to the priest which is necessary to secure validity.

In the same way, the use of sacred vestments which are reserved to priests or deacons (stoles, chasubles or dalmatics) at liturgical ceremonies by non-ordained members of the faithful is clearly unlawful.

Every effort must be made to avoid even the appearance of confusion which can spring from anomalous liturgical practices. As the sacred ministers are obliged to wear all of the prescribed liturgical vestments, so too the non-ordained faithful may not assume that which is not proper to them.

To avoid any confusion between sacramental liturgical acts presided over by a priest or deacon, and other acts which the non-ordained faithful may lead, it is always necessary to use clearly distinct ceremonials, especially for the latter.

Article 7

Sunday Celebrations in the Absence of a Priest

§ 1. In some places in the absence of priests or deacons,[90] non-ordained members of the faithful lead Sunday celebrations. In many instances, much good derives for the local community from this useful and delicate service when it is discharged in accordance with the spirit and the specific norms issued by the competent ecclesiastical authority.[91] A special mandate of the bishop is necessary for the non-ordained members of the faithful to lead such celebrations. This mandate should contain specific instructions with regard to the term of applicability, the place and conditions in which it is operative, as well as indicate the priest responsible for overseeing these celebrations.

§ 2. It must be clearly understood that such celebrations are temporary solutions and the text used at them must be approved by the competent ecclesiastical authority.[92] The practice of inserting into such celebrations elements proper to the Holy Mass is prohibited. So as to avoid causing error in the minds of the faithful,[93] the use of the Eucharistic prayers even in narrative

---

90. Cf. *ibid.*, canon 1248, § 2.

91. Cf. *ibid.*, canon 1248, § 2: Sacred Congregation for Rites, Instruction *Inter Oecumenici* (Sept. 26, 1964), 37: *AAS* 66 (1964), p. 885; Sacred Congregation for Divine Worship, *Directorium de Celebrationibus Dominicalibus Absente Presbytero, Christi Ecclesia* (June 10, 1988), *Notitiae* 263 (1988).

92. Cf. John Paul II, *Address ad Quosdam Americae Septemtrionalis Episcopos Sacra Limina Visitantes* (June 5, 1993): *AAS* 86 (1994), p. 340.

93. Sacred Congregation for Divine Worship, *Directorium de Celebrationibus Dominicalibus Absente Presbytero, Christi Ecclesia* (June 10, 1988), 35: *loc. cit.;* cf. also *C.I.C.*, canon 1378, § 2, 1° and § 3; canon 1384.

form at such celebrations is forbidden. For the same reasons, it should be emphasized for the benefit of those participating, that such celebrations cannot substitute for the Eucharistic sacrifice and that the obligation to attend Mass on Sunday and holydays of obligation is satisfied only by attendance at Holy Mass.[94] In cases where distance or physical conditions are not an obstacle, every effort should be made to encourage and assist the faithful to fulfill this precept.

ARTICLE 8

The Extraordinary Minister of Holy Communion

The non-ordained faithful already collaborate with the sacred ministers in diverse pastoral situations since: "This wonderful gift of the Eucharist, which is the greatest gift of all, demands that such an important mystery should be increasingly better known and its saving power more fully shared."[95]

Such liturgical service is a response to the objective needs of the faithful, especially those of the sick, and to those liturgical assemblies in which there are particularly large numbers of the faithful who wish to receive Holy Communion.

§ 1. The canonical discipline concerning *extraordinary ministers of Holy Communion* must be correctly applied so as to avoid generating confusion. The same discipline establishes that the ordinary minister of Holy Communion is the bishop,

94. Cf. *C.I.C.*, canon 1248.

95. Sacred Congregation for the Discipline of the Sacraments, Foreword of the Instruction *Immensae Caritatis* (Jan. 29, 1973): *AAS* 65 (1973), p. 264.

the priest and the deacon.[96] Extraordinary ministers of Holy Communion are those instituted as acolytes and the faithful so deputed in accordance with canon 230, § 3.[97]

A non-ordained member of the faithful, in cases of true necessity, may be deputed by the diocesan bishop, using the appropriate form of blessing for these situations, to act as an extraordinary minister to distribute Holy Communion outside of liturgical celebrations *ad actum vel ad tempus* or for a more stable period. In exceptional cases or in unforeseen circumstances, the priest presiding at the liturgy may authorize such *ad actum.*[98]

§ 2. Extraordinary ministers may distribute Holy Communion at Eucharistic celebrations only when there are no ordained ministers present or when those ordained ministers present at a liturgical celebration are truly unable to distribute Holy Communion.[99] They may also exercise this function at Eucharistic celebrations where there are particularly large numbers of the faithful and which would be excessively prolonged because of an insufficient number of ordained ministers to distribute Holy Communion.[100]

---

96. 5 Cf. *C.I.C.,* canon 910, § 1; cf. John Paul II, Letter *Dominicae Cenae* (Feb. 24, 1980), 11; *AAS* 72 (1980), p. 142.

97. Cf. *C.I.C.,* canon 910, § 2.

98. Cf. Sacred Congregation for the Discipline of the Sacraments, Instruction *Immensae Caritatis* (Jan. 29, 1973): *AAS* 65 (1973), p. 264, n. 1; *Missale Romanum,* Appendix: *Ritus ad Deputandum Ministrum S. Communionis ad Actum Distribuendae; Pontificale Romanum, De Institutione Lectorum et Acolythorum.*

99. Pontifical Commission for the Authentic Interpretation of the Code of Canon Law, *Response* (June 1, 1998): *AAS* 80 (1988), p. 1373.

100. Cf. Sacred Congregation for the Discipline of the Sacraments, Instruction *Immensae Caritatis* (Jan. 29, 1973), 1: *AAS* 65 (1973), p. 264;

This function is *supplementary and extraordinary*[101] and must be exercised in accordance with the norm of law. It is thus useful for the diocesan bishop to issue particular norms concerning extraordinary ministers of Holy Communion which, in complete harmony with the universal law of the Church, should regulate the exercise of this function in his diocese. Such norms should provide, among other things, for matters such as the instruction in Eucharistic doctrine of those chosen to be extraordinary ministers of Holy Communion, the meaning of the service they provide, the rubrics to be observed, the reverence to be shown for such an august sacrament and instruction concerning the discipline on admission to Holy Communion.

To avoid creating confusion, certain practices are to be avoided and eliminated where such have emerged in particular Churches:

—extraordinary ministers receiving Holy Communion apart from the other faithful as though concelebrants;

—association with the renewal of promises made by priests at the Chrism Mass on Holy Thursday, as well as other categories of the faithful who renew religious vows or receive a mandate as extraordinary ministers of Holy Communion;

—the habitual use of extraordinary ministers of Holy Communion at Mass, thus arbitrarily extending the concept of "a great number of the faithful."

Sacred Congregation for the Sacraments and Divine Worship, Instruction *Inaestimabile Donum* (April 3, 1980), 10: *AAS* 72 (1980), p. 336.

101. Canon 230, § 2 and § 3 *C.I.C.*, affirms that the liturgical services can be assigned to non-ordained faithful only *"ex temporanea deputatione"* or for supply.

ARTICLE 9

The Apostolate to the Sick

§ 1. In this area, the non-ordained faithful can often provide valuable collaboration.[102] Innumerable works of charity to the sick are constantly provided by the non-ordained faithful either individually or through community apostolates. These constitute an important Christian presence to the sick and suffering of the greatest importance. The non-ordained faithful particularly assist the sick by being with them in difficult moments, encouraging them to receive the sacraments of Penance and the Anointing of the Sick, by helping them to have the disposition to make a good individual confession as well as to prepare them to receive the Anointing of the Sick. In using sacramentals, the non-ordained faithful should ensure that these are in no way regarded as sacraments whose administration is proper and exclusive to the bishop and to the priest. Since they are not priests, in no instance may the non-ordained perform anointings either with the oil of the sick or any other oil.

§ 2. With regard to the administration of this sacrament, ecclesiastical legislation reiterates the theologically certain doctrine and the age-old usage of the Church[103] which regards

102. Cf. *Rituale Romanum—Ordo Unctionis Infirmorum,* Praenotanda, 17: Editio Typica, 1972.

103. Cf. Jas 5:14-15; St. Thomas Aquinas, *In IV Sent.* d. 4, q. 1; Ecumenical Council of Florence, bull *Exsultate Deo (DS* 1325); Ecumenical Council of Trent, *Doctrina de Sacramento Extremae Unctionis,* chapter 3 *(DS* 1697, 1700) and canon 4; *De Extrema Unctione (DS* 1719); *Catechism of the Catholic Church,* 1516.

the priest as its only valid minister.[104] This norm is completely coherent with the theological mystery signified and realized by means of priestly service.

It must also be affirmed that the reservation of the ministry of Anointing to the priest is related to the connection of this sacrament to the forgiveness of sin and the worthy reception of the Holy Eucharist. No other person may act as ordinary or extraordinary minister of the sacrament since such constitutes simulation of the sacrament.[105]

ARTICLE 10

Assistance at Marriages

§ 1. The possibility of delegating the non-ordained faithful to assist at marriages may prove necessary in special circumstances where there is a grave shortage of sacred ministers.

This possibility, however, is subject to the verification of three conditions. The diocesan bishop may concede this delegation only in cases where there are no priests or deacons available, and after he shall have obtained for his own diocese a favorable *votum* from the conference of bishops and the necessary permission of the Holy See.[106]

§ 2. In such cases, the canonical norms concerning the validity of delegation,[107] the suitability, capacity and attitude of the non-ordained faithful must be observed.[108]

---

104. Cf. *C.I.C.*, canon 1003, § 1.

105. Cf. *ibid.*, canons 1379 and 392, § 2.

106. Cf. *ibid.*, canon 1112.

107. Cf. *ibid.*, canon 1111, § 2.

108. Cf. *ibid.*, canon 1112, § 2.

§ 3. With the exception of an extraordinary case due to the absolute absence of both priests and deacons who can assist at marriages provided for in canon 1112 of the Code of Canon Law, no ordained minister may authorize the non-ordained faithful for such assistance. Neither may an ordained minister authorize the non-ordained faithful to ask or receive matrimonial consent according to the norm of canon 1108, § 2.

ARTICLE 11

The Minister of Baptism

Particularly praiseworthy is the faith with which many Christians, in painful circumstances of persecution, or in missionary territories or in special cases of necessity, have afforded and continue to afford the sacrament of Baptism to new generations of Christians in the absence of ordained ministers.

Apart from cases of necessity, canonical norms permit the non-ordained faithful to be designated as extraordinary ministers of Baptism[109] should there be no ordinary minister or in cases where he is impeded.[110] Care should be taken, however, to avoid too extensive an interpretation of this provision, and such a faculty should not be conceded in a habitual form.

Thus, for example, that absence or the impediment of a sacred minister which renders licit the deputation of the lay faithful to act as an extraordinary minister of Baptism, cannot

109. Cf. *ibid.*, canon 861, § 2; *Ordo Baptismi Parvulorum,* Praenotanda Generalia, nn. 16-17.

110. Cf. *ibid.*, canon 230.

be defined in terms of the ordinary minister's excessive workload, or his non-residence in the territory of the parish, nor his non-availability on the day on which the parents wish the Baptism to take place. Such reasons are insufficient for the delegation of the non-ordained faithful to act as extraordinary ministers of Baptism.

ARTICLE 12

Leading the Celebration at Funerals

In the present circumstances of growing dechristianization and of abandonment of religious practice, death and the time of obsequies can be one of the most opportune pastoral moments in which the ordained minister can meet with the non-practicing members of the faithful.

It is thus desirable that priests and deacons, even at some sacrifice to themselves, should preside personally at funeral rites in accordance with local custom, so as to pray for the dead and be close to their families, thus availing of an opportunity for appropriate evangelization.

The non-ordained faithful may lead the ecclesiastical obsequies provided that there is a true absence of sacred ministers and that they adhere to the prescribed liturgical norms.[111] Those so deputed should be well prepared both doctrinally and liturgically.

111. Cf. *Ordo Exsequiarum*, Praenotanda, 19.

Article 13

Necessary Selection and Adequate Formation

Should it become necessary to provide for "supplementary" assistance in any of the cases mentioned above, the competent authority is bound to select lay faithful of sound doctrine and exemplary moral life. Catholics who do not live worthy lives or who do not enjoy good reputations or whose family situations do not conform to the teaching of the Church may not be admitted to the exercise of such functions. In addition, those chosen should possess that level of formation necessary for the discharge of the responsibilities entrusted to them.

In accordance with the norms of particular law, they should perfect their knowledge particularly by attending, insofar as possible, those formation courses organized for them by the competent ecclesiastical authority in the particular Churches,[112] (in environments other than that of the seminary, as this is reserved solely for those preparing for the priesthood).[113] Great care must be exercised so that these courses conform absolutely to the teaching of the ecclesiastical Magisterium and they must be imbued with a true spirituality.

---

112. Cf. *C.I.C.*, canon 231, § 1.

113. By this is meant "seminary" situations where laity and those preparing for the priesthood receive the same education and formation together, as though both were destined for the same ministry. Such "seminaries" have sometimes been called "integrated" or "mixed."

CONCLUSION

The Holy See entrusts this present document to the pastoral zeal of diocesan bishops in the various particular Churches, and to other ordinaries in the hope that its application may produce abundant fruit for the growth, in communion, of sacred ministers and the non-ordained faithful.

The Holy Father reminds us: "The particular gift of each of the Church's members must be wisely and carefully acknowledged, safeguarded, promoted, discerned and coordinated, without confusing roles, functions or theological and canonical status."[114]

While on the one hand the numerical shortage of priests may be particularly felt in certain areas, on the other, it must be remembered that in other areas there is currently a flowering of vocations which augurs well for the future. Solutions addressing the shortage of ordained ministers cannot be other than transitory and must be linked to a series of pastoral programs

---

114. John Paul II, Discourse at the Symposium on "The Participation of the Lay Faithful in the Priestly Ministry" (May 11, 1994), 3: *loc. cit.*

which give priority to the promotion of vocations to the sacrament of Holy Orders.[115]

In this respect the Holy Father notes that in "some local situations, generous, intelligent solutions have been sought. The legislation of the Code of Canon Law has itself provided new possibilities which, however, must be correctly applied, so as not to fall into the ambiguity of considering as ordinary and normal, solutions that were meant for extraordinary situations in which priests were lacking or in short supply."[116]

The object of this document is to outline specific directives to ensure the effective collaboration of the non-ordained faithful in such circumstances, while safeguarding the integrity of the pastoral ministry of priests. "It should also be understood that these clarifications and distinctions do not stem from a concern to defend clerical privileges but from the need to be obedient to the will of Christ, and to respect the constitutive form which he indelibly impressed on his Church."[117]

The correct application of these same directives, in the context of a living hierarchical *communion,* is advantageous to the lay faithful who are called to develop the rich potentiality of their specific identity and the "ever greater willingness to live it so as to fulfill one's proper mission."[118]

The impassioned appeal which the Apostle to the nations addresses to Timothy: "I charge you in the sight of God and Jesus Christ...to preach the Word, be urgent in season and out

---

115. Cf. *ibid.,* 6.

116. *Ibid.,* 2.

117. *Ibid.,* 5.

118. John Paul II, Post-Synodal Apostolic Exhortation *Christifideles Laici* (Dec. 30, 1988), 58: *loc. cit.,* p. 507.

of season; reprove, entreat, rebuke.... Be watchful in all things, fulfill your ministry" (2 Tim 4:1-5), which applies in a special way to the sacred pastors who are called by office, "to foster the discipline which is common to the whole Church...pressing for the observance of all ecclesiastical laws."[119]

This grave duty constitutes a necessary means by which the richness present in every state of ecclesial life can be correctly conformed to the promptings of the Spirit, and by which *communion* becomes an effective reality in the daily journeying of the entire community.

May the Blessed Virgin Mary, Mother of the Church, to whose intercession this document is commended, assist all in understanding its purpose, and bring to fruitful completion those efforts, made in apostolic concern, to apply it faithfully.

All particular laws, customs and faculties conceded by the Holy See *ad experimentum* or by other ecclesiastical authorities which are contrary to the foregoing norms are hereby revoked.

The Supreme Pontiff, in audience of the 13th of August, 1997, approved in forma specifica *this present Instruction and ordered its promulgation.*

Vatican City
August 15, 1997

The Solemnity of the Assumption
of the Blessed Virgin Mary

119. *C.I.C.,* canon 392.

Congregation for the Clergy

Darío Castrillón Hoyos
Pro-Prefect

Crescenzio Sepe
Secretary

Pontifical Council for the Laity

James Francis Stafford
President

Stanislaw Rylko
Secretary

Congregation for the Doctrine of the Faith

Joseph Card. Ratzinger
Prefect

Tarcisio Bertone, SDB
Secretary

Congregation for Divine Worship and the Discipline of the Sacraments

Jorge Arturo Medina Estévez
Pro-Prefect

Geraldo Majella Agnelo
Secretary

Congregation for Bishops

Bernardin Card. Gantin
Prefect

Jorge María Mejía
Secretary

Congregation for the Evangelization of Peoples

Jozef Card. Tomko
Prefect

Giuseppe Uhac
Secretary

Congregation for Institutes of Consecrated Life and Societies of Apostolic Life

Eduardo Card. Martínez Somalo
Prefect

Piergiorgio Silvano Nesti, CP
Secretary

Pontifical Council for the Interpretation of Legislative Texts

Julián Herranz Casado
President

Bruno Bertagna
Secretary

The Daughters of St. Paul operate book and media centers at the following addresses. Visit, call or write the one nearest you today, or find us on the World Wide Web, www.pauline.org

CALIFORNIA
3908 Sepulveda Blvd., Culver City, CA 90230; 310-397-8676
5945 Balboa Ave., San Diego, CA 92111; 619-565-9181
46 Geary Street, San Francisco, CA 94108; 415-781-5180

FLORIDA
145 S.W. 107th Ave., Miami, FL 33174; 305-559-6715

HAWAII
1143 Bishop Street, Honolulu, HI 96813; 808-521-2731

ILLINOIS
172 North Michigan Ave., Chicago, IL 60601; 312-346-4228

LOUISIANA
4403 Veterans Memorial Blvd., Metairie, LA 70006; 504-887-7631

MASSACHUSETTS
Rte. 1, 885 Providence Hwy., Dedham, MA 02026; 781-326-5385

MISSOURI
9804 Watson Rd., St. Louis, MO 63126; 314-965-3512

NEW JERSY
561 U.S. Route 1, Wick Plaza, Edison, NJ 08817; 732-572-1200

NEW YORK
150 East 52nd Street, New York, NY 10022; 212-754-1110
78 Fort Place, Staten Island, NY 10301; 718-447-5071

OHIO
2105 Ontario Street, Cleveland, OH 44115; 216-621-9427

PENNSYLVANIA
9171-A Roosevelt Blvd., Philadelphia, PA 19114; 215-676-9494

SOUTH CAROLINA
243 King Street, Charleston, SC 29401; 803-577-0175

TENNESEE
4811 Poplar Ave., Memphis, TN 38117; 901-761-2987

TEXAS
114 Main Plaza, San Antonio, TX 78205; 210-224-8101

VIRGINIA
1025 King Street, Alexandria, VA 22314; 703-549-3806

CANADA
3022 Dufferin Street, Toronto, Ontario, Canada M6B 3T5; 416-781-9131
1155 Yonge Street, Toronto, Ontario, Canada M4T 1W2; 416-934-3440

¡Libros en español!